Climate Holocaust

H.H. Friedrich

Table of Contents

Introduction

In the year 2004 the victims of insufficient climate action abound. With heatwaves hitting 50 Celsius for weeks at a time, HUNDREDS die from heatstroke, MILLIONS are displaced, and lower primates fall off dead from the trees. But NEVERMORE, to the previous demands of climate action we now demand as well climate justice at all levels. Justice will prevail!!!

It is essential to:

- STOP animal agriculture
- STOP deep sea fishing.
- STOP food waste.
- STOP deforestation
- STOP fossil fuels
- STOP plastics production

temple
- Jaime Lagún

Global Perspective: The daily climate reports cover diverse regions affected by climate change, highlighting its worldwide impact.

Scientific Validation: This book doesn't just present the problem; it clearly outlines solutions and demands action from governments and financial institutions.

Emphasis on Inequality: The report highlights the disproportionate impact of climate change on vulnerable populations and calls for wealthier nations to bear their share of responsibility.

Areas for Further Discussion:

Mitigation vs. Adaptation: While the report emphasizes adaptation measures like the Loss and Damage Fund, it could also explore the crucial role of mitigating climate change through emissions reduction.

Geopolitics: The report mentions the COPs and negotiations but could benefit from deeper analysis of the political hurdles hindering progress on climate action.

Solutions: While the report calls for clean energy and financial support, it could delve further into specific policy recommendations or technological innovations.

Future Scenarios: The report could explore potential future scenarios if climate change continues unchecked, providing a more comprehensive picture of the risks.

Overall, this report serves as a powerful call to action, effectively conveying the severity of climate change and the urgent need for global cooperation to address it.

Chapter 1

A World on Fire: The Human Cost of the 2024 Heatwaves and Droughts

The year 2024 will be etched in history as a stark reminder of the brutal reality of climate change. Across the globe, a tapestry of suffering unfolded as unprecedented heatwaves and crippling droughts gripped vast swathes of land, leaving behind a trail of human misery that defies words. This essay will delve into the scientific evidence that confirms the link between these extreme events and human-induced climate change, while also exposing the horrifying consequences for the people caught in the crosshairs of this planetary crisis.

The 2024 heatwaves were not mere anomalies. They were driven by a complex interplay of forces, with human-induced climate change playing a central role. The Earth's atmosphere, saturated with greenhouse gases, traps more heat, leading to hotter temperatures and intensifying heatwaves. The scientific consensus is unequivocal: human activity is the dominant driver of the observed warming trend. This is evident in the relentless rise of global average temperatures, with 2024 setting new records, further amplified by natural climate variations like El Niño.

These soaring temperatures, however, are not just statistics on a chart. They translate into a visceral experience of suffering for millions. In India, temperatures soared above 50 degrees Celsius, pushing the limits of human endurance. Across Europe, wildfires raged out of control, fuelled by tinder-dry conditions, consuming homes and displacing communities. In California, the relentless heat exacerbated a long-term drought, stretching water resources to their breaking point. From the scorched fields of the American Midwest to the parched lands of Africa, the story remained the same: a struggle for survival against the forces of a rapidly warming planet.

The suffering goes far beyond the physical discomfort of heat. Heatwaves lead to a cascade of cascading effects:

Health Impacts: Heatstroke, dehydration, and respiratory problems are exacerbated, leading to a surge in hospital admissions and tragically, an increase in heat-related deaths.

The elderly, children, and those with underlying health conditions are particularly vulnerable.

Agricultural Collapse: The foundations of food security crumble under the pressure of extreme heat and drought. Crops wither and fail, livestock perish, and food prices skyrocket, pushing millions into hunger and poverty.

Water Scarcity: Dwindling water reserves intensify water stress, leading to conflicts, social unrest, and displacement. The struggle for access to clean water becomes a daily battle for survival.

Economic Devastation: Heatwaves and droughts cripple infrastructure, disrupt industries, and force businesses to close, leading to unemployment and financial ruin. The economic consequences are far-reaching, disproportionately impacting the most vulnerable communities.

It is important to recognize that the suffering is not evenly distributed. The most vulnerable populations, often those who have contributed the least to climate change, are the hardest hit. In developing countries, lack of access to basic resources, infrastructure, and healthcare exacerbates the impact of extreme events. The global south, burdened by historical inequities and economic disparities, finds itself on the frontlines of a crisis it did not create.

The 2024 heatwaves and droughts are not simply a natural phenomenon; they are a stark warning. They are a reflection of our collective failure to address the climate crisis with the urgency it demands. The scientific evidence is irrefutable, the human cost is immeasurable, and the time for action is now.

The road ahead requires a fundamental shift in our approach. We must transition away from fossil fuels, invest in renewable energy, and prioritize adaptation measures to build resilience to future extreme events. We must recognize the interconnectedness of our planet and the shared responsibility we all bear in tackling this challenge. The suffering witnessed in 2024 should serve as a wake-up call, urging us to act with courage, compassion, and urgency to avert a future where the human cost of climate change is far greater than we can imagine.

Chapter 2

A Costly Reality: One Trillion and Counting - A Requiem for a Planet in Peril

The world is not just warming; it is broiling. The once-abstract concept of climate change has become a brutal reality, etched into the fabric of our lives through catastrophic weather events, rising sea levels, and the silent displacement of millions. This "costly reality," as a recent report chillingly proclaims, is no longer a matter of speculation but a quantifiable crisis – one that has already surpassed the staggering threshold of a trillion dollars in damage.

This report, a powerful testament to the urgency of our situation, goes beyond mere statistics to paint a vivid picture of a world in distress. It uses concrete examples, like the devastating floods that ravaged Pakistan in 2022, leaving behind a trail of destruction estimated at $30 billion, to illustrate the tangible consequences of climate change. This approach moves beyond the realm of theoretical projections and brings the reality of climate impacts to our doorstep.

The report's strength lies in its global perspective, showcasing the universality of this crisis. From the searing heat waves in Europe to the intensifying droughts in Africa, the report underscores how no region is immune to the ramifications of a warming planet. This global lens reveals the interconnectedness of our world and the urgent need for coordinated global action.

Further reinforcing the gravity of the situation, the report emphasizes the scientific consensus linking these events to climate change. It cites the work of leading climate scientists and research institutions, adding a layer of scientific validity to its claims. This not only strengthens its credibility but also dispels any lingering doubts about the anthropogenic nature of climate change.

The report doesn't shy away from calling for action. It urges governments and financial institutions to acknowledge the escalating costs of climate change and to act decisively to mitigate its impact. It highlights the need for a global framework, such as the Loss and Damage Fund, to support vulnerable communities most acutely affected by climate change. This emphasis on equitable solutions is crucial, recognizing the disproportionate burden placed on developing nations despite their minimal contribution to the problem.

However, the report's focus on adaptation, while necessary, underscores the need for deeper exploration of mitigation strategies. While adapting to a changing climate is critical, we cannot ignore the fundamental need to reduce emissions and limit further warming. This requires a concerted global effort to transition to renewable energy sources, implement ecological practices, and address the systemic issues driving our dependence on fossil fuels.

Moreover, the report's brief mention of political hurdles in international climate negotiations necessitates a more in-depth analysis of the geopolitical complexities hindering progress. Understanding the political landscape, the competing interests, and the historical context surrounding these negotiations is crucial to crafting effective solutions.

Finally, while the report provides a strong call for action, it would benefit from a more detailed examination of specific policy recommendations and technological innovations. Exploring concrete solutions, such as carbon pricing mechanisms, green financing initiatives, or advanced climate modeling tools, would empower policymakers and stakeholders to translate the report's warnings into tangible actions.

The report concludes by outlining the stark realities of an unchecked climate crisis. It compels us to contemplate the future scenarios that await us if we fail to act decisively. By painting a vivid picture of potential societal disruptions, economic collapse, and mass displacement, the report serves as a powerful wake-up call to humanity.

"One Trillion and Counting" is a poignant reminder that the cost of inaction is immeasurable. It is a clarion call for global cooperation, bold leadership, and immediate action. The future of our planet rests on our ability to confront this "costly reality" with courage, innovation, and a collective commitment to safeguarding the future of our shared home.

Chapter 3

The Science of Attribution: Linking Extreme Weather to Climate Change

The world is witnessing a dramatic increase in the frequency and intensity of extreme weather events – from devastating heatwaves and wildfires to catastrophic floods and storms. As these events wreak havoc on human lives, infrastructure, and ecosystems, a crucial question arises: Is climate change responsible? The science of attribution provides a powerful tool to answer this question, offering a deeper understanding of the role human-induced climate change plays in these extreme weather events.

The Fundamental Principle:

Attribution science relies on the fundamental principle that human activities, primarily the emission of greenhouse gases, are altering the Earth's climate system. This alteration manifests in various ways, including rising global temperatures, changing precipitation patterns, and increased atmospheric moisture. These changes create a new baseline for weather events, making certain extremes more likely or more intense.

A Multifaceted Approach:

Attribution science employs a multifaceted approach, drawing upon a combination of observational data, climate models, and statistical methods. By comparing observed weather data with simulations from climate models, scientists can discern the influence of human-induced climate change on specific events. These models incorporate various factors, such as greenhouse gas emissions, natural climate variability, and solar radiation, allowing for a comprehensive analysis.

The Power of Statistical Analysis:

Statistical analysis plays a crucial role in attributing specific events to climate change. Scientists use various statistical techniques, including Bayesian statistical methods, to calculate the probability of an event occurring in a world with climate change versus a world without it. The results are often expressed as "likelihood ratios," quantifying the relative likelihood of the event occurring in a changed climate.

Examples of Attributed Events:

Numerous studies have successfully attributed extreme weather events to climate change. For example, the devastating 2021 heatwave that scorched the Pacific Northwest was found to be virtually impossible without human-induced climate change. Similarly, the 2017 Hurricane Harvey, which caused widespread flooding in Houston, was found to be significantly more intense due to climate change.

Beyond Individual Events:

Attribution science not only focuses on individual events but also investigates broader trends. By analyzing a series of events, scientists can identify patterns and determine how climate change is affecting the frequency and intensity of specific types of extreme weather. For instance, studies have shown that climate change is increasing the likelihood of droughts in certain regions and intensifying heatwaves globally.

Implications and Importance:

The science of attribution has profound implications for understanding the impacts of climate change and informing adaptation and mitigation strategies. By demonstrating the clear link between human activities and extreme weather, attribution science provides compelling evidence for the urgency of addressing climate change. This knowledge empowers policymakers, communities, and individuals to take proactive steps to prepare for and mitigate the risks associated with extreme weather events.

Conclusion:

Attribution science provides a powerful and increasingly sophisticated tool for understanding the role of climate change in extreme weather events. By employing a combination of observational data, climate models, and statistical analysis, scientists can confidently identify the fingerprints of climate change on specific events and broader trends. This knowledge is vital for informed decision-making, enabling us to better prepare for a future shaped by a changing climate. As we continue to grapple with the increasing frequency and intensity of extreme weather events, the science of attribution will continue to play a crucial role in guiding our understanding and response.

Chapter 4

The Global North's Debt: A Legacy of Exploitation and the Looming Climate Crisis

The Earth groans under a weight of its own making. The 2024 heatwaves, droughts, and floods are not isolated events but potent symptoms of a deeper, systemic crisis - one born from a history of unchecked exploitation and a refusal to acknowledge the interconnectedness of our planet. The Global North, with its long history of colonialism and industrialization, bears a heavy responsibility for this crisis. It is time to address the debt owed, not in dollars, but in genuine action and commitment to a more equitable future.

The Global North's dominance has been built on the exploitation of the Global South. From the transatlantic slave trade to the extraction of resources, the Global North has profited immensely at the expense of the South, leaving behind a trail of devastation. The very industries that fueled the North's economic boom – fossil fuel extraction, deforestation, and large-scale agriculture – have laid the groundwork for the climate crisis we now face. The Global South, despite contributing minimally to the problem, is bearing the brunt of the consequences, experiencing disproportionate suffering from extreme weather events, rising sea levels, and disrupted ecosystems.

The 2024 heatwaves, droughts, and floods are stark reminders of this reality. The unprecedented heatwaves in Europe and North America, the crippling droughts in Africa and the Middle East, and the devastating floods in South Asia are not mere natural occurrences. They are the direct result of anthropogenic climate change, amplified by the historical injustices inflicted on the Global South. The carbon footprint of the Global North, accumulated over centuries of unrestrained industrialization, has triggered a cascade of consequences, disproportionately impacting those who have contributed least to the problem.

The current debt owed by the Global North is not merely financial. It is a debt of responsibility, a moral obligation to address the systemic inequalities that have fueled the climate crisis. This debt must be acknowledged and addressed with concrete action. This requires a paradigm shift, moving beyond the narrow focus on economic growth and embracing a ecological development model that prioritizes environmental justice and equitable resource distribution.

Here are some crucial steps the Global North can take to begin repaying its debt:

Radical decarbonization: The Global North must rapidly transition to renewable energy sources and implement ambitious policies to reduce emissions. This requires a shift away from fossil fuel dependence and investment in clean energy infrastructure.

Financial reparations: The Global North must provide substantial financial assistance to the Global South to adapt to climate impacts and build resilience. This should involve debt cancellation, technology transfer, and direct financial support for climate mitigation and adaptation projects.

Climate justice advocacy: The Global North must actively support climate justice movements and demand accountability from corporations and governments for their role in the climate crisis. This includes holding polluters responsible for their actions and ensuring a fair and equitable future.

The 2024 heatwaves, droughts, and floods are a wake-up call. We are at a crossroads. The Global North has a critical opportunity to acknowledge its historical responsibility, act with urgency, and work collaboratively with the Global South to build a more just and absolutely ecological future. Failing to do so would only perpetuate the cycle of exploitation and ensure that future generations will face an even more catastrophic reality. The future of our planet hinges on our collective willingness to recognize the debt owed and act with resolute commitment to a climate-just world.

Chapter 5

Vulnerable Populations: Bearing the Brunt of the Climate Crisis

The Earth's climate is undergoing a period of rapid and unprecedented change, driven primarily by human activity. This change manifests as rising global temperatures, shifting precipitation patterns, more extreme weather events, and rising sea levels. While these impacts affect everyone, they are felt most acutely by vulnerable populations - those already facing systemic disadvantages and disparities in resource access.

These populations, often marginalized by socioeconomic factors, geography, and ethnicity, bear the brunt of the climate crisis in ways that disproportionately exacerbate existing inequalities. The climate crisis amplifies pre-existing vulnerabilities, creating a cascade of interconnected challenges:

1. Food Security and Agricultural Impacts: Climate change disrupts agricultural practices, impacting yields and threatening food security. Drought, floods, and extreme temperatures directly impact crop production, while shifting weather patterns threaten

livestock and disrupt vital ecosystems. This directly impacts vulnerable populations, who often rely on subsistence agriculture for their livelihood and food.

2. Water Scarcity and Sanitation: Changing rainfall patterns exacerbate water scarcity, particularly in arid and semi-arid regions. Droughts lead to water shortages, impacting drinking water access, sanitation, and food production, disproportionately affecting marginalized communities with limited access to clean water and sanitation infrastructure.

3. Health Impacts: Extreme weather events, heat waves, and air pollution stemming from climate change exacerbate existing health problems. Vulnerable populations, often lacking access to healthcare and living in environments with higher exposure to pollutants, are particularly susceptible to respiratory illnesses, heat-related illnesses, and infectious diseases.

4. Displacement and Migration: Rising sea levels, extreme weather events, and degradation of natural resources lead to displacement and forced migration. Coastal communities, particularly in low-lying areas, face the most immediate threat, with their livelihoods and homes at risk. This displacement

disproportionately impacts vulnerable populations, who lack the resources and support networks to adapt and relocate effectively.

5. Economic Disparity and Social Inequality: Climate change disproportionately impacts economic sectors reliant on natural resources, further marginalizing already vulnerable populations. This creates a vicious cycle, perpetuating poverty and hindering access to resources, education, and healthcare, ultimately perpetuating social and economic inequalities.

6. Gender Inequality and Social Justice: Climate change disproportionately affects women and girls, who are often responsible for water collection, food production, and childcare. Their vulnerability is further amplified by limited access to resources, education, and decision-making power, making it harder for them to adapt to climate change impacts.

Addressing the Vulnerability:

The challenge lies in recognizing and addressing these interconnected vulnerabilities. Social justice, and climate action must be intertwined to ensure a just future.

Here are some critical steps:

Empowering Vulnerable Populations: Providing access to information, resources, and technology, including early warning systems, climate-smart agricultural practices. This involves investing in education, skills development, and community-based initiatives.

Addressing Systemic Inequalities: Tackling underlying social, economic, and political inequalities that perpetuate vulnerability to climate change. This includes addressing discrimination, promoting gender equality, and ensuring equal access to resources and services.

Building Resilience: Supporting community-based initiatives and traditional knowledge systems to build resilience against climate change impacts. This includes promoting diversification of livelihoods, strengthening social networks, and investing in disaster preparedness.

Investing in Climate Adaptation and Mitigation: Directing resources to climate adaptation measures that protect vulnerable populations, including proper water management, resilient infrastructure, and disaster risk reduction. Additionally, prioritizing climate mitigation efforts, such as reducing greenhouse gas emissions, to lessen the severity of future impacts.

International Collaboration and Justice: Strengthening international cooperation and collaboration, including equitable access to climate finance and technology transfer. This also involves acknowledging the historical responsibility of developed nations in causing climate change and supporting developing nations in their adaptation and mitigation efforts.

The climate crisis is a global challenge that requires a collective response. Addressing the specific vulnerabilities faced by marginalized communities is crucial for achieving climate justice. By prioritizing equity, resilience, and collaborative action, we can mitigate the impacts of climate change and build a more equitable world for generations to come.

Chapter 6

Beyond Insurance: The Hidden Costs of Climate Disasters

The specter of climate change looms large, casting a shadow of uncertainty over our future. While the immediate impact of extreme weather events is often measured in terms of property damage and financial losses, the true cost of climate disasters stretches far beyond insurance claims. This essay delves into the hidden, cascading costs that ripple through society, highlighting the profound economic, social, and ecological repercussions of our changing climate.

The Economic Tsunami:

The financial impact of climate disasters goes beyond immediate insurance payouts. Disrupted supply chains, halted economic activity, and the costs of reconstruction all contribute to a prolonged economic downturn. Take, for instance, Hurricane Katrina. While the estimated insured losses were around $40 billion, the total economic impact exceeded $100 billion, considering lost productivity, business closures, and long-term infrastructure repair. This highlights the stark difference between the insured and the true economic costs, a discrepancy that only widens as climate change intensifies.

Beyond immediate economic losses, climate disasters also impact long-term economic growth. The constant fear of recurring disasters can deter investment, hinder economic development, and create a cycle of perpetual rebuilding. This becomes particularly relevant in developing nations where the infrastructure and resources are less resilient, making them more vulnerable to climate impacts.

Social Scars and Human Suffering:

The social impact of climate disasters is equally devastating, leaving behind a legacy of trauma and displacement. The loss of homes, livelihoods, and communities can lead to mental health issues, social unrest, and increased vulnerability to exploitation. For example, the displacement caused by the droughts in the Sahel region has fueled conflict and instability, highlighting the interconnectedness of climate change, social unrest, and human suffering.

The health implications are equally profound. Extreme heat events, floods, and droughts can trigger heatstrokes, respiratory illnesses, and waterborne diseases, increasing the burden on already strained healthcare systems. Climate change exacerbates existing health disparities, disproportionately affecting marginalized communities with limited access to resources and support.

The Ecological Ripple Effect:

The ecological consequences of climate disasters are far-reaching and complex. Degradation of ecosystems, loss of biodiversity, and disruption of natural cycles all contribute to a spiraling environmental crisis. For instance, coral bleaching caused by rising ocean temperatures not only decimates marine life but also disrupts vital ecosystems that support a vast array of species.

Climate disasters also accelerate deforestation and land degradation, further exacerbating climate change through the release of stored carbon. This cycle of destruction creates a feedback loop, amplifying the severity and frequency of extreme weather events and perpetuating a vicious cycle of ecological decline.

Moving Beyond the Visible:

The hidden costs of climate disasters are a stark reminder of the multifaceted nature of this global challenge. It's not simply about replacing damaged buildings or compensating for lost income. It's about addressing the long-term social, economic, and ecological consequences that permeate every aspect of our lives.

Moving forward, we must shift our focus beyond immediate insurance claims and embrace a comprehensive approach that incorporates the hidden costs. This requires:

Investing in resilience: Building resilient infrastructure, developing early warning systems, and promoting adaptive practices to minimize the impact of future disasters.

Strengthening social safety nets: Providing support to vulnerable communities and addressing health disparities to mitigate the social consequences of climate change.

Promoting truly just practices: Implementing policies and technologies that reduce greenhouse gas emissions and protect natural resources to address the root cause of the crisis.

The hidden costs of climate disasters are not a distant threat, but a reality that demands our urgent attention. We must acknowledge the profound impact beyond the visible and act with courage and determination to build a wonderful future.

Chapter 7

The Loss and Damage Fund: A Critical Step Towards Climate Justice

The Earth's climate is changing at an unprecedented rate, driven by human-induced greenhouse gas emissions. This change manifests in increasingly extreme weather events, rising sea levels, and cascading ecological disruptions, disproportionately impacting vulnerable populations across the globe. The devastating consequences of these climate impacts, often termed "loss and damage," present a stark moral and ethical imperative to address the inequalities inherent in climate change. The establishment of a dedicated Loss and Damage Fund at COP27 marks a critical step towards acknowledging this reality and achieving climate justice.

The Global Divide in Climate Change Impacts:

The reality of climate change is a story of two worlds. Developed nations, historically responsible for the majority of greenhouse gas emissions, are generally better equipped to adapt to and mitigate climate impacts. However, developing nations, despite having contributed minimally to the problem, bear the brunt of its consequences. These countries, often located in geographically vulnerable regions, lack the resources and infrastructure to adapt to the increasing frequency and intensity of extreme weather events, resulting in significant loss of life, displacement, and damage to infrastructure and livelihoods.

The Loss and Damage Fund: A Long-Overdue Recognition of Climate Justice:

The Loss and Damage Fund, agreed upon at COP27, represents a long-awaited recognition of the unequal burden of climate change. It signifies a shift in the global narrative, acknowledging the need for concrete financial support to address the irreversible impacts already experienced by vulnerable communities. This commitment is not merely about providing aid; it is about ensuring climate justice by acknowledging historical responsibility and providing support for adaptation and recovery efforts.

Beyond Financial Support: A Multifaceted Approach to Climate Justice:

The establishment of the Fund is a crucial first step, but achieving true climate justice requires a multifaceted approach. Alongside financial resources, this includes:

Enhanced Transparency and Accountability: Clear guidelines and mechanisms are necessary to ensure the Fund is effectively managed and that resources reach the most vulnerable communities.

Strengthening Climate Resilience: Investing in adaptation measures, such as early warning systems, drought-resistant crops, is essential to build resilience and minimize future losses.

Addressing Root Causes: The Fund must be seen as a catalyst for ambitious climate action. Developed nations must significantly increase their commitments to emissions reduction to prevent further escalation of climate impacts.

Empowering Local Communities: The design and implementation of the Fund should prioritize local ownership and participation, ensuring that solutions are tailored to the specific needs and contexts of vulnerable communities.

The Road Ahead: Challenges and Opportunities:

The journey towards a just and equitable response to climate change will not be without challenges. The Fund's operationalization, including funding mechanisms and governance structures, requires careful consideration and consensus among stakeholders. However, the creation of the Loss and Damage Fund presents a unique opportunity to:

Build Trust and Solidarity: The Fund has the potential to foster greater trust and collaboration between developed and developing nations, paving the way for more effective global climate action.

Be ecological. By supporting adaptation and recovery, the Fund can contribute to the achievement of a resilient future.

Shift the Global Paradigm: The Fund serves as a powerful symbol of the growing global recognition of climate justice, setting a precedent for future efforts to address the inequalities inherent in climate change.

Conclusion:

The Loss and Damage Fund is a vital step towards acknowledging the reality of climate injustice and addressing the unequal burden of climate change impacts. It represents a commitment to solidarity and shared responsibility, recognizing the imperative to support vulnerable communities and a better reality.

Chapter 8

Decentralized Renewables: Harnessing Clean Energy for an Ecological Future

The Earth's climate is changing, and the consequences are becoming increasingly evident. From rising sea levels and extreme weather events to melting glaciers and disrupted ecosystems, the need for immediate action is undeniable. The transition to a noncarbon energy future hinges on embracing decentralized renewables – a paradigm shift that promises not only clean energy but also enhanced resilience, equitable access, and economic opportunity.

The Case for Decentralization:

The traditional centralized model of energy production relies on large-scale power plants, often fueled by fossil fuels, and a vast network of transmission lines. This model suffers from inherent vulnerabilities:

Single Points of Failure: Centralized power plants are susceptible to natural disasters, cyberattacks, and other disruptions, causing widespread blackouts.

Inefficient Transmission: Long-distance transmission losses can be significant, reducing energy efficiency and increasing costs.

Limited Accessibility: Rural communities and areas with weak infrastructure often lack access to reliable electricity.

Environmental Impact: Large-scale power plants contribute to air pollution, land degradation, and water scarcity.

Decentralized renewables offer a compelling alternative. They involve generating and consuming electricity closer to the point of use, utilizing renewable energy sources like solar, wind, and hydro. This approach tackles the shortcomings of the centralized model by:

Boosting Resilience: Distributed generation reduces reliance on a single grid and increases local energy security.

Improving Efficiency: Minimizing transmission distances lowers losses and enhances overall energy efficiency.

Expanding Access: Decentralized systems make clean energy accessible to even remote communities, promoting equitable development.

Reducing Environmental Impact: By utilizing renewable resources, decentralized systems contribute to a cleaner, healthier environment.

Technological Advancements:

The rapid advancements in renewable energy technology have been crucial in enabling decentralized solutions. These advancements include:

Solar Photovoltaic (PV) Technology: Improved efficiency and reduced costs have made solar PV panels increasingly affordable and accessible.

Wind Turbine Technology: Advances in wind turbine design and blade technology have significantly increased efficiency and reduced noise pollution.

Energy Storage Solutions: Battery technology is rapidly evolving, allowing for the efficient storage of renewable energy and providing grid stability.

Smart Grid Technologies: Advanced grid management systems enable intelligent integration of decentralized renewable sources.

Economic and Social Benefits:

Decentralized renewables offer substantial economic and social benefits:

Job Creation: The deployment and maintenance of decentralized systems create local jobs, boosting regional economies.

Energy Independence: Decentralization fosters energy independence by reducing reliance on fossil fuels and imported energy.

Community Empowerment: Local ownership and control of energy resources empower communities and promote economic development.

Reduced Energy Poverty: Expanding access to clean energy improves living standards and reduces energy poverty, particularly in underserved communities.

Challenges and Opportunities:

The transition to a decentralized renewables future is not without its challenges:

Regulatory Frameworks: Existing regulations often hinder the widespread adoption of decentralized renewables.
Grid Integration: Integrating distributed energy sources requires robust grid management systems and smart technologies.

Financing and Investment: Securing financing and investment for decentralized projects can be challenging, especially for small-scale projects.

These challenges are best addressed through collaborative efforts involving policymakers, energy providers, technology developers, and communities.

The Path Forward:

Achieving an ecological future requires a comprehensive strategy:

Policy Support: Governments need to create enabling policies that promote decentralized renewables, including tax incentives, feed-in tariffs, and streamlined permitting processes.

Technological Innovation: Continuous innovation in renewable energy technologies and storage solutions is essential for further cost reductions and improved performance

Community Engagement: Active community participation is crucial for the successful implementation and ownership of decentralized energy projects.

Infrastructure Development: Investment in smart grids and energy storage infrastructure is vital for integrating decentralized renewable sources seamlessly.

Conclusion:

Decentralized renewables represent a transformative approach to energy production and consumption. By embracing this paradigm shift, we can harness clean energy for a one health future, one that is resilient, equitable, and prosperous. The transition to a decentralized renewables future will require a collective effort involving all stakeholders – governments, businesses, and communities – working together to build a cleaner world for generations to come.

Chapter 9

Taxing Polluters: Funding Climate Action Through Equitable Measures

The climate crisis is an undeniable reality, manifesting in increasingly frequent and severe extreme weather events, rising sea levels, and disruptions to ecosystems. Addressing this crisis requires a multifaceted approach, but at its core lies a fundamental principle: those responsible for the problem should bear the cost of its solution. This is where "taxing polluters" emerges as a potent and equitable strategy for funding climate action.

The Moral Imperative: The current model of economic growth, heavily reliant on fossil fuels, has been built on a foundation of externalities – costs not accounted for in market prices. The burning of fossil fuels, for example, has contributed significantly to climate change, leading to devastating consequences for vulnerable populations and future generations. Taxing polluters acknowledges the moral imperative of holding those responsible for these externalities accountable.

Fairness and Equity: Implementing a carbon tax in conjunction with targeted investments in vulnerable communities and programs that address the disproportionate impacts of climate change on marginalized groups ensures equity. Revenues generated through a carbon tax can fund social safety nets, climate adaptation initiatives, and research and development for clean energy technologies. This approach not only tackles climate change but also addresses the inequalities exacerbated by its consequences.

International Cooperation: A global carbon pricing system would create a common ground for international cooperation in addressing climate change. By aligning incentives across borders, such a system could incentivize emissions reduction globally.

Practical Implementation: Implementing a carbon tax effectively requires careful consideration of several key aspects. Firstly, the tax must be sufficiently high to incentivize real behavioral change and generate substantial revenue. Secondly, a transparent and efficient system for collecting and utilizing the tax revenue is crucial. Thirdly, the design must be sensitive to the needs of vulnerable communities and industries that might face disproportionate burdens.

Addressing Concerns: Some argue that carbon taxes disproportionately burden low-income households. This concern can be mitigated through targeted policies such as direct rebates or investments in clean energy infrastructure that benefit low-income communities. Others argue that it could lead to job losses in polluting industries. This can be addressed by investing in retraining programs and promoting the growth of green sectors, creating new employment opportunities.

Conclusion: Taxing polluters is a moral imperative, an efficient strategy, and a key element of a just and ecological future. By internalizing the true cost of pollution and channeling the revenue towards climate action and social equity, a carbon tax can serve as a catalyst for transformative change. It is time to shift the paradigm from rewarding pollution to rewarding responsible environmental stewardship, ensuring a future that represents total health.

Chapter 10

Investing in Resilience: Building Climate-Proof Communities

The Earth is not just warming - it is broiling. This statement, once a scientific hypothesis, is now an undeniable reality, fueled by human activity and shaping the future of our planet. The consequences are already being felt globally, from increasingly frequent and severe heatwaves, droughts, and floods to rising sea levels and intensifying storms. These impacts are not abstract; they are devastating communities, disrupting livelihoods, and forcing millions to relocate. The need to adapt and build resilience is no longer a choice, but a moral and practical imperative.

This essay will explore the crucial concept of "climate-proof communities," examining the multifaceted strategies and investments required to build resilient infrastructure, foster social cohesion, and empower communities to navigate the challenges of a changing climate.

Beyond Adaptation: Building Resilience

The term "adaptation" often implies a reactive approach, a response to the immediate threat of climate change. While necessary, adaptation alone is insufficient. We must move beyond reactive measures and embrace the concept of "resilience," a proactive and transformative approach that strengthens communities against future shocks and stresses.

The Pillars of Resilience:

A climate-proof community is not merely one that withstands climate impacts, but one that thrives despite them. This requires a multi-faceted approach, encompassing three key pillars:

1. Infrastructure for a Changing Climate: Investing in robust infrastructure that can withstand extreme weather events is fundamental. This includes:

Proper water management: Developing reliable water sources, enhancing water storage systems, and implementing efficient water usage practices to mitigate drought and flooding.

Climate-resilient infrastructure: Designing and constructing buildings, roads, and other infrastructure to withstand extreme weather events and adapt to rising sea levels.

Noncarbon energy systems: Diversifying energy sources, investing in renewable energy technologies, and strengthening power grids to ensure uninterrupted power supply during disasters.

2. Social Cohesion and Inclusive Development: Building resilience requires strong community bonds, diverse participation, and equitable access to resources. This involves:

Early warning systems: Establishing effective communication channels and community-based early warning systems to disseminate crucial information and prepare for impending events.

Social safety nets: Implementing social safety nets, such as disaster relief funds and insurance programs, to support vulnerable communities and provide financial assistance in times of crisis.

Capacity building and knowledge sharing: Equipping communities with the skills, knowledge, and resources to adapt to climate change, including disaster preparedness training, ecological agricultural practices, and risk assessment methods.

3. Empowering Local Communities: Community-driven approaches are crucial for successful adaptation and resilience building. This means:

Decentralized decision-making: Fostering participatory decision-making processes where local communities are empowered to shape and implement climate-resilient solutions that address their unique needs.

Indigenous knowledge integration: Recognizing and valuing the traditional knowledge and practices of indigenous communities, which often hold valuable insights into climate change adaptation and disaster risk reduction.

Building local capacity: Investing in local capacity building initiatives that empower communities to identify, analyze, and address climate-related challenges.

The Economic Case for Resilience:

Investing in resilience is not a cost, but an investment in the future. It generates significant economic returns by mitigating the economic losses associated with climate impacts. A resilient community is a more productive community, better able to withstand shocks and maintain economic stability. This translates to:

Reduced economic losses from climate-related disasters: Investing in robust infrastructure and early warning systems can significantly reduce damage and economic disruptions caused by extreme weather events.

Enhanced economic productivity: Climate-resilient communities are better equipped to thrive, attracting investment and fostering Wellbeing.

Increased agricultural productivity: Ecologicble agricultural practices and water management strategies can enhance agricultural yields and food security.

A Call to Action:

Building climate-proof communities is a global challenge requiring collective action. Governments, businesses, civil society organizations, and communities must work together to:

Increase funding for climate adaptation and resilience building: Prioritizing investments in resilience projects and increasing funding for climate adaptation programs is essential.

Develop and implement climate-resilient policies and regulations: Establishing strong policies that promote safe and respectful infrastructure, green building codes, and disaster risk reduction measures is crucial.

Promote collaboration and knowledge sharing: Facilitating collaboration between different stakeholders, sharing best practices, and disseminating knowledge on resilience building are key.

Empower first nations: Supporting community-led initiatives, strengthening local governance structures, and ensuring equitable access to resources are vital.

The future is not predetermined. By investing in resilience, we can navigate the challenges of a changing climate and create a future where communities thrive, not just survive.

Chapter 11

COPs and Negotiations: The Challenges of Global Climate Governance

The world's climate is changing, with consequences that are already being felt across the globe. From rising sea levels and extreme weather events to disruptions in agricultural yields and biodiversity loss, the impacts of climate change are undeniable. This stark reality has spurred a global effort to address the issue through international cooperation, culminating in the annual Conference of the Parties (COPs) under the United Nations Framework Convention on Climate Change (UNFCCC). Yet, despite decades of negotiations and ambitious pronouncements, the progress made towards achieving a healthy future at all levels remains frustratingly slow. This essay will delve into the challenges hindering effective global climate governance, focusing on the intricacies of COP negotiations and the complexities of achieving consensus amongst diverse stakeholders with differing priorities and interests.

The very structure of the COPs, designed to foster consensus through multilateral diplomacy, presents inherent challenges. The "common but differentiated responsibilities" principle, enshrined in the UNFCCC, acknowledges the historical contribution of developed nations to global emissions and their greater capacity to mitigate climate change. This principle, however, leads to ongoing tensions and disputes over the allocation of responsibilities and financial commitments. Developed nations often resist pressure to increase their commitments, while developing nations, facing pressing economic and developmental priorities, struggle to balance their own needs with the urgency of climate action.

The negotiations themselves are fraught with complexities. COPs involve a multitude of stakeholders, including governments, non-governmental organizations, businesses, and civil society groups, each with their own perspectives and priorities. This diverse representation can make consensus-building a laborious process, often leading to protracted negotiations and compromises that dilute ambitious targets. The "bottom-up" approach, relying on individual nations to submit their own Nationally Determined Contributions (NDCs), while offering flexibility, can also undermine the effectiveness of global efforts, as individual pledges may fall short of the collective ambition needed to limit global warming to well below 2 degrees Celsius, as per the Paris Agreement.

Furthermore, the issue of climate finance remains a contentious sticking point. Developed nations have pledged to mobilize $100 billion annually by 2020 to support climate action in developing countries, but this commitment has consistently fallen short. The lack of transparency and accountability in the delivery of climate finance further exacerbates the mistrust between developed and developing nations, undermining the credibility of global climate governance.

Beyond the immediate challenges, the complexity of climate change presents a fundamental obstacle to effective governance. Climate change is a global issue with diverse and interconnected impacts, requiring solutions that transcend national boundaries. This complexity necessitates a shift in thinking, moving beyond narrow national interests to embrace a truly global perspective. It requires acknowledging the interconnectedness of ecosystems, recognizing the disproportionate impacts on vulnerable populations, and embracing a long-term vision that prioritizes intergenerational equity and the preservation of the planet for future generations.

Despite the challenges, the COPs remain a critical platform for global climate governance. The ongoing negotiations offer an opportunity to bridge divides, foster collaboration, and develop mechanisms for effective implementation. The success of the COPs hinges on a commitment to multilateralism, a willingness to compromise, and a shared understanding of the urgency and gravity of the climate crisis. The future of our planet depends on it.

Chapter 12

Geopolitics of Climate Change: Navigating Power Dynamics and Interests

Climate change is no longer a distant threat; it is a present reality shaping global power dynamics and geopolitical interests. The interconnectedness of our planet means that the consequences of climate change, from rising sea levels to extreme weather events, are felt universally, but not equally. This essay examines the intricate web of power dynamics and competing interests that emerge as nations navigate the existential crisis of a warming world.

Unequal Burden, Unequal Power: The very nature of climate change exacerbates existing global inequalities. Developing nations, often the least responsible for historical greenhouse gas emissions, are disproportionately vulnerable to the impacts of climate change. Coastal communities in low-lying nations face the prospect of displacement, agricultural productivity plummets in regions experiencing droughts, and water scarcity intensifies existing conflicts. This uneven distribution of vulnerability creates a complex geostrategic landscape where the consequences of inaction fall heavily on the shoulders of those with the least capacity to adapt.

The Geopolitical Dance: Climate change presents a unique challenge, forcing nations to confront their own interests in the context of a shared planetary future. This necessitates a departure from traditional geopolitical calculations, where national security is primarily defined by military strength. Climate security, in contrast, requires a multifaceted approach encompassing resource management, technological innovation, and collaborative governance.

The Scramble for Resources: As climate change impacts resource availability, the competition for access to essential resources like water, food, and energy will intensify. This fuels geopolitical tensions, as nations seek to secure their own interests amidst dwindling resources. For instance, the melting Arctic ice cap has opened up new shipping routes and access to untapped oil and gas reserves, leading to increased territorial claims and potential conflict.

The Quest for Climate Leadership: The response to climate change has also created new avenues for power projection. Nations with technological prowess, financial resources, and policy leadership are vying to shape the global response to climate change. This struggle for climate leadership involves not only technological advancement and financial support for mitigation and adaptation efforts but also the framing of global narratives and international agreements.

The Dilemma of Collaboration: While international cooperation is essential to address climate change effectively, achieving consensus across diverse interests remains a major challenge. National self-interest often clashes with the need for collective action, leading to a complex dance of negotiation, compromise, and strategic positioning. This tension is evident in global climate negotiations, where conflicting priorities, historical responsibilities, and differing levels of ambition often impede progress.

The Rise of Climate Diplomacy: The growing importance of climate change has spurred the emergence of climate diplomacy as a key component of foreign policy. This involves bilateral and multilateral negotiations, the development of climate-related agreements, and the strengthening of international institutions dedicated to climate action. Climate diplomacy requires careful balancing of national interests with global imperatives, fostering dialogue and understanding between nations with diverging perspectives.

The Role of Non-State Actors: Climate change transcends national borders and impacts the lives of individuals and communities worldwide. This has led to the rise of non-state actors, including civil society organizations, businesses, and indigenous communities, as crucial players in climate action. These actors often advocate for ambitious climate policies, raise awareness, and promote innovative solutions, injecting new perspectives and pressures into the geopolitical landscape.

Navigating the Path Forward: Addressing the geopolitics of climate change demands a multi-pronged approach. It requires acknowledging the uneven distribution of vulnerability and working towards equitable solutions that address the needs of the most vulnerable populations. It necessitates a shift in thinking towards climate security as a core component of national security, fostering international cooperation and collaboration. This will involve prioritizing collective action, building resilience, and fostering a sense of shared responsibility for the future of our planet.

Conclusion: The geopolitics of climate change is a complex and dynamic field, characterized by competing interests, power dynamics, and the urgency for global cooperation. Navigating this landscape requires a deep understanding of the interconnectedness of climate change, resource availability, security, and the evolving role of non-state actors.

Chapter 13

Tipping Points and Feedback Loops: A Bleak Future Without Action

The Earth, a vibrant tapestry of interconnected systems, is delicately balanced on the precipice of irreversible change. While we often perceive the environment as a static backdrop, it is, in fact, a dynamic web of feedback loops and tipping points, perpetually adjusting to the pressures we impose. It is within this intricate framework that the terrifying truth of our current predicament emerges: inaction in the face of climate change will not merely result in a warmer planet, but a cascade of cascading failures, ushering in a bleak future for humanity.

Imagine a domino effect, where the fall of one domino triggers the fall of many others. This is the essence of tipping points, thresholds beyond which ecosystems can no longer withstand the pressure and shift into a new, often drastically different, state. The melting of Arctic sea ice is a prime example. As ice melts, it exposes darker ocean surfaces, which absorb more sunlight, further accelerating the melting process. This vicious cycle, a positive feedback loop, amplifies the initial perturbation, pushing the system towards a new equilibrium – a world devoid of Arctic sea ice.

The impacts of such shifts extend far beyond the immediate region. A diminished Arctic ice cap disrupts global weather patterns, alters ocean currents, and increases sea levels, threatening coastal communities worldwide. This is just one example of how interconnected our planet is. As one system shifts, it triggers changes in others, creating a domino effect of cascading failures.

The Amazon rainforest, a vital carbon sink, faces a similar threat. Deforestation, driven by human activities, reduces the rainforest's capacity to absorb carbon dioxide, further accelerating climate change. This escalating pressure, coupled with drought and rising temperatures, increases the risk of a catastrophic tipping point where the rainforest transitions from a lush ecosystem to a barren savanna. This transition would unleash a torrent of consequences: loss of biodiversity, diminished rainfall, increased soil erosion, and a surge in greenhouse gas emissions, further intensifying climate change.

The consequences of these tipping points are not confined to the natural world. They have profound implications for human civilization. Food security, water resources, and human health will be severely impacted by climate change. Rising sea levels will displace millions, while extreme weather events will become more frequent and intense, leading to mass migrations, economic instability, and social unrest.

The scientific consensus is clear: the window of opportunity to avoid catastrophic climate change is rapidly closing. The longer we delay action, the more likely we are to trigger irreversible tipping points, setting in motion a cascade of events that will reshape our planet and our future.

This is not a call for despair, but a rallying cry for action. We must recognize the interconnectedness of our planet and the perilous consequences of inaction. By understanding the concept of tipping points and feedback loops, we can grasp the urgency of the situation and act decisively to mitigate the climate crisis. The future of our planet and our civilization hinges on our collective will to embrace an ecological path, leaving behind a legacy of responsible stewardship for generations to come.

Chapter 14

A World Transformed: The Path to Climate Resilience

The Earth, our planet, is in a state of profound transformation. Driven by the relentless march of human activity, the climate is changing at an unprecedented rate, threatening to unravel the very fabric of life as we know it. We stand at a crossroads, faced with a stark choice: to passively accept the consequences of our actions, or to actively shape a future that is fully resilient. This essay delves into the critical issues surrounding climate change, explores the path to achieving climate resilience, and emphasizes the urgency and the profound responsibility we bear as stewards of this planet.

The Urgency of Climate Change: The scientific evidence is overwhelming: our planet is warming, and the consequences are far-reaching. Rising global temperatures are melting glaciers and ice sheets, causing sea levels to rise and threaten coastal communities. Extreme weather events, such as hurricanes, droughts, and wildfires, are becoming more frequent and severe, displacing populations and disrupting ecosystems. The impact of climate change extends far beyond physical changes; it disrupts food security, exacerbates social inequalities, and threatens global stability.

Building Climate Resilience: A Multifaceted Approach: Achieving climate resilience requires a fundamental shift in our approach to the environment and a commitment to transformational change. This involves a multifaceted strategy encompassing the following key areas:

1. Mitigation: Reducing Greenhouse Gas Emissions: At the heart of tackling climate change lies the imperative to reduce greenhouse gas emissions. This requires a transition to clean energy sources like solar, wind, and geothermal, coupled with a dramatic reduction in fossil fuel consumption. Stop using animals as a source of food (see the “Cowspiracy” documentary). Stop deep sea fishing (See the “Seaspiracy” documentary).

Moreover, investing in energy efficiency, promoting ecological transportation systems, and implementing policies that incentivize low-carbon practices are crucial steps.

2. Adaptation: Building Resilient Communities and Infrastructure: Climate change is already impacting our world, and its effects will continue to intensify in the coming decades. Therefore, adaptation strategies are essential to minimize the negative impacts and enhance our capacity to cope with climate-related risks. This includes building resilient infrastructure, implementing early warning systems for extreme weather events, developing drought-resistant crops, and promoting respectful land management practices.

3. Development: Integrating Environmental, Economic, and Social Considerations: The pursuit of climate resilience cannot be achieved in isolation. It necessitates a holistic approach to development that prioritizes the environment while addressing social and economic needs. This means fostering a circular economy, investing in renewable resources, promoting equitable access to resources, and ensuring that no one is left behind in the transition to a low-carbon future.

The Role of Technology and Innovation: Technological innovation plays a pivotal role in the path to climate resilience. New technologies can help us monitor and predict climate change, develop cleaner energy sources, optimize resource utilization, and adapt to the changing environment. Investing in research and development, fostering collaboration between academia, industry, and governments, and facilitating the adoption of new technologies are essential to accelerate progress.

A Collective Effort: The challenge of climate change is not one that can be solved by any single nation, organization, or individual. It requires a global effort, built on cooperation, collaboration, and a shared sense of responsibility. International agreements, such as the Paris Agreement, provide a framework for collective action, while individual nations and communities must implement policies and initiatives that align with these global goals.

The Future is in Our Hands: The path to climate resilience is not a linear one; it involves challenges, setbacks, and constant adaptation. But it is a path that we must embrace, for the sake of our planet and future generations. By acknowledging the urgency of the situation, committing to ambitious goals, and harnessing the power of innovation and cooperation, we can create a world that is not only resilient to climate change but also just, equitable. The future is in our hands, and the time for action is now.

Once again, It is essential to:

- STOP animal agriculture
- STOP deep sea fishing.
- STOP food waste.
- STOP deforestation
- STOP fossil fuels
- STOP plastics production

In the meantime trillions of dollars should be paid in full to the global south.

be treated as a
temple
- Jaime

We DEMAND Climate Justice NOW

We DEMAND Climate Action NOW

www.ingramcontent.com/pod-product-compliance
Lightning Source LLC
LaVergne TN
LVHW060824170826
845678LV00010B/1898

* 9 7 9 8 2 3 0 2 4 7 2 8 9 *